Original title:
The Orchard's Promise

Copyright © 2025 Creative Arts Management OÜ
All rights reserved.

Author: Adeline Fairfax
ISBN HARDBACK: 978-1-80586-418-9
ISBN PAPERBACK: 978-1-80586-890-3

Whispers in the Apple Blossoms

In the branches, laughter flies,
Wiggly worms wear silly ties.
Bees buzz jokes from flower to flower,
Tickling petals within the hour.

A squirrel dons a cap so bright,
Claiming apples as his right.
While birds chirp silly little tunes,
Dancing 'neath the fluffy moons.

Beneath the Boughs of Secrets

Napping gnomes in leafy beds,
Snoring soft with funny heads.
Crickets squeak in treetop bands,
Playing tunes with tiny hands.

Pinecones giggle, topsy-turvy,
While the daisies act all swirly.
A mystic apple dreams of pie,
Wondering who will give it a try.

Harvesting Dreams at Dusk

As shadows lengthen, apples roll,
Chasing each other, that's their goal.
A raccoon stacks apples in a pile,
Hoping for a fruity style.

Lettuce giggles in the breeze,
Competing in a dance with ease.
While the moon winks from the skies,
Conspiring with the fireflies.

Petals of Hope in Shaded Light

Under leaves, the grass tickles toes,
Laughter erupts as the fun grows.
A gopher spins in dizzy loops,
Claiming apples as his troops.

While butterflies juggle on a whim,
Stars above begin to swim.
A full moon grins with glimmering light,
Inviting all to dance tonight.

Illuminated Paths of Promise

Beneath the trees, the shadows shift,
A squirrel scurries, oh what a gift!
With apples so shiny, it's hard to resist,
They always seem brighter, so hard to miss.

The branches bow low, a casual embrace,
While bees do a tango, all over the place.
The laughter of leaves, a comedic duet,
Nature's own comedy, the best you can get.

The Fragrance of Anticipated Joy

The blossoms are winking, can you smell the cheer?
A duck's doing ballet, right over here!
Each blossom a joke, each fruit a surprise,
While snails hold a meeting under wise blue skies.

Sipping sweet nectar, the hummingbirds play,
As butterflies gossip in a colorful way.
With laughter so bright, the sun shows his grin,
And even the worms tap dance, jumping in!

Renewal in Every Seedling's Crest

Tiny green sprouts, brave little chaps,
Spreading their charm as they wiggle and clap.
With roots full of giggles, they push through the dirt,
Thinking their job is to make the world flirt!

The wise old oak chuckles, a gentleman bold,
As tales of their growth begin to unfold.
Each sprout is a joker, just biding its time,
Ready to burst forth with laughter in rhyme.

Echoes of Sunlight on the Grasses

The sun spills its laughter, a golden cascade,
Dancing on grasses, a shimmering parade.
With shadows that giggle, they twist and they prance,
Even the flowers seem caught in a dance.

A frog leaps and croaks, his own little tune,
While ants stage a play under the watchful moon.
In this field of cheer, every crack is a joke,
As nature sends forth a joyous bespoke!

Fruits of Tomorrow's Embrace

In the garden where dreams reside,
A tomato wearing a flashy slide.
The apple is planning a daring race,
While the grapes giggle all over the place.

A pear with a hat and shoes so bright,
Takes a leap, what a funny sight!
Bananas are slipping, oh what a fall,
Laughing together, they cover it all.

Beneath Canopies of Time

Under leaves with a shady grin,
A coconut dreams of a spin to win.
Oranges arm wrestle, zest in the air,
As cherries play poker without a care.

Time ticks slowly with giggles and cheers,
While limes tell stories from yesteryear.
Beneath branches where secrets extend,
The humor of nature, our joyful friend.

Seasons Woven in Gold

Winter wears a cloak made of zest,
While spring shows off its colorful fest.
Berries are bustling, making their plans,
As nuts tell tales but get stuck in cans.

Summer sizzles with laughter so loud,
Watermelons jump in a giggling crowd.
Autumn joins in with a playful gust,
Telling each fruit, 'In fun, we trust!'

Scent of Sunlit Futures

In the early light, bananas conspire,
Dreaming of smoothies, their heart's desire.
Melons with laughter bounce on the floor,
Whilst figs take moments to ponder and roar.

With a peel of delight, they dance in a row,
Each one proclaiming, 'Just watch us grow!'
The scent of bright sun meets the crunch of a bite,
In this fruity future, everything's right!

An Evening Reverie in the Grove

In a grove where shadows play,
The squirrels dance the night away.
With acorns flying through the air,
My hat has vanished—oh, beware!

A raccoon steals my picnic feast,
While laughing like a cheeky beast.
The fireflies hold a wacky race,
Their tiny lights a silly chase.

The trees are swaying, quite a sight,
As crickets chirp with sheer delight.
I trip on roots, I feel so spry,
But then I see the moon—oh my!

The night concludes with laughter loud,
As owls hoot madly, oh so proud.
In the grove, I'll raise a glass,
To nights like this—what a gas!

Of Seasons Shifting and Souls Awakening

Spring arrives with silly hats,
As bunnies hop like acrobats.
Flowers giggle, petals bright,
They chat about the morning light.

Summer brings a sunburned grin,
As popsicle drips slide down my chin.
The bees are buzzing off their tune,
I swear, they're cha-cha dancing soon!

Autumn sings in colors bold,
With leaves that twirl like stories told.
The pumpkins grinning in the park,
They're planning mischief after dark.

Winter woes with icy slides,
The snowmen play with arms so wide.
With snowball fights and frosty cheer,
Each season brings a laugh, oh dear!

Whimsy in Each Blossoming Petal

In the garden, tarts abound,
Where sugary blooms are found.
A cookie tree, a chocolate vine,
I swear this place is quite divine!

The daisies giggle in the breeze,
While ladybugs play hide-and-seek with ease.
A butterfly on a sugar spree,
Sipping nectar from a cup of tea.

As petals fall like tiny stars,
I bump my head on candy bars.
The watermelon plants grow big and round,
As fruit confetti falls to the ground.

In this garden of quirky sights,
Laughter blooms on sunny nights.
Each petal whispers secrets sweet,
Where whimsy and delight shall meet!

In the Arms of Leafy Embrace

In the garden, fruits will fall,
A pear once danced, now hit the wall.
The apples giggle, plump and round,
While cherries play hide and seek on the ground.

A squirrel peers in, donuts in mind,
Stealing snacks of a juicy kind.
The lemons frown, they're stuck in a tree,
While orange slices plot to break free.

The Lure of a Hidden Harvest

Beneath the leaves, a cucumber hides,
Whispering secrets where no one glides.
The melons think they're the kings of the patch,
While zucchinis just grin, waiting to hatch.

Grasshoppers leap with style and flair,
Critics claim they're hip, we don't care!
A pumpkin once painted himself so bright,
He startled the squash in the dead of night.

Between the Rows of Time

Through the rows where veggies grow tall,
Carrots swipe at each other's sprawl.
Lettuce laughs at the turnip's stare,
While beans introduce themselves with flair.

A beet tries to dance, but trips on a sprout,
"No worries," it cheers, with a berry in doubt.
Tomatoes squabble over shade to rest,
While radishes dream of being the best.

A Celebration of Life's Cycles

In spring, the buds pop like little caps,
While worms throw a party with joyful claps.
The sun's a comedian, with rays to share,
As shadows creep, giggles fill the air.

Summer brings laughter, oh what a sight,
With bees buzzing tunes, a pure delight.
The harvest parade attracts all the crowd,
And veggies perform, all humble and loud.

Sun-Kissed Days of Abundance

Bouncing apples, red and round,
Rolling off the ground with sound.
Squirrels plotting with a grin,
They schemed a heist to get them in!

Juicy peaches hanging low,
Giggles shared with tasty flow.
A fruit fight starts, oh what fun!
Who knew lunch could be a run?

Grapes are bouncing, one, two, three,
Caught in a laughter symphony.
Cherry pits are flying high,
Like little rockets through the sky!

Sunset comes, amid the cheer,
We dance with fruit, we've no fear.
In orchard shade, we'll laugh and play,
With dreams of bugs in disarray!

The Journey of Each Falling Petal

A petal sways, it takes a dive,
Flutters down, it feels alive.
Landing quick, what a show!
"Catch me if you can!" – they go!

Whirling laughs as petals race,
Catching air, in wild embrace.
Spinning tales upon the ground,
Each turn a giggle, each twist a sound!

Pollen pirates on a spree,
Planning pranks with glee and glee.
"Steal a snack!" one did proclaim,
As daisies joined the wacky game!

Evening falls, their journey done,
Petals rest, but not for fun.
In dreams they twirl, alive with zest,
Expecting mischief, oh the best!

A Canvas of Changing Seasons

Winter's chill made snowflakes spin,
But goofy birds jumped in the din.
Chasing flakes, they twirled in flight,
"Snowball fight!" they chirped with delight.

Springtime blooms with colors bright,
Blossoms burst, a fabulous sight!
Bees start buzzing, looking confused,
"Do we pollinate or dance?" they mused!

Summer sun, a melting scene,
With popsicles bright and ice cream keen.
Kids chase shadows, giggling loud,
Splashing in puddles, feeling proud!

Fall arrives, leaves whirl with flair,
"Crunch, crunch!" echoes, a leaf affair.
Squirrels stuff their cheeks full,
"Harvest dance!" they joyfully pull!

Tales of Roots and Wings

Roots that giggle, deep in the ground,
"Tickle me!" they laugh all around.
Wings of blooms, a fluttery joke,
"Who needs soil? I'd rather float!"

Comets of dandelions soar,
Kids chase puffs, hungry for more.
"Make a wish!" one shouts in glee,
As petals spin, wild and free.

In trees they gossip, branches wide,
"Who's the best?" they laugh and bide.
"Let's bet on who will swing the most!"
The flowers giggle, sipping toast!

Even as seasons change their tune,
The roots and wings are never strewn.
They share their stories, heartfelt cheer,
In this garden, laughter's near!

Fruits of Forgotten Dreams

In a tree where dreams take flight,
Lemons talk with all their might.
Mangoes laugh at endless schemes,
Bananas slide in sunshine beams.

Cherries giggle in the breeze,
Whispering secrets to the bees.
Plums juggle thoughts of pie and jam,
While apples plot a silly slam.

The pears decide to form a band,
With fig-leaves clapping, oh so grand.
But in the end, they rest and play,
Dreaming of what they'll be someday.

Blossoms Under a Gilded Sky

Sunflowers wear their shades of gold,
While daisies laugh, or so I'm told.
Petals dance on breezes light,
Underneath the stars so bright.

Pomegranates play leapfrog games,
Whimsical with their funny names.
Oranges rocket through the air,
While grapes declare, "Life's not fair!"

The garden's full of chatter and cheer,
Even weeds join in, oh dear!
With laughter echoing all around,
In this silly sight, joy is found.

Beneath the Canopy of Hope

Beneath the leaves that wink and sway,
Lemons and limes plot their wild play.
Coconuts bounce on soft green grass,
While berries form a raucous class.

Peaches wear their fuzzy hats,
Debating fiercely with chitchatting brats.
Kiwis giggle, bright and green,
While dreaming of their big cuisine.

The mango prances with delight,
Inventing games that last all night.
In this garden, laughs ignite,
Fruits frolic till the morning light.

Harvest of the Heart's Desire

When the sun spills honey on the ground,
Witty pumpkins giggle, round and brown.
Carrots wear sunglasses on their sides,
And rhubarb sports the daftest rides.

On harvest day, the fruits all cheer,
Wasting time, oh what a year!
Cabbages roll like daring fools,
While mushrooms run their secret schools.

With rhymes and puns in this wild feast,
Even the trees join in, at least!
Together they sing a jolly tune,
Celebrating beneath the moon.

The Sweetness of Ripened Days

In the sun, the fruits do laugh,
Their skins glow red, like a little gaffe.
A squirrel steals one, runs up a tree,
Dancing as if it were wild and free.

The bees buzz round in a goofy race,
With sticky feet, they're all over the place.
A peach falls down, and oh what a sight,
It bounces back up — oh, what a fright!

The apples joke about being round,
While somewhere a melon refuses to sound.
Each day brings giggles from the vine,
As laughter ripens in the sunshine.

Who knew fruit could have so much fun?
In this jolly patch, we'll never be done.
With every bite, a chortle plays,
In this blissful, ripened maze.

Where Roots Embrace the Earth

Down below, the roots do meet,
In a ticklish dance, they tap their feet.
They wiggle madly in their earthy lair,
Saying, 'We live without a care!'

The worms join in, with squirmy flair,
Doing the cha-cha without a care.
While tiny seeds giggle in the ground,
Waiting for sun, they all gather round.

The beetles boast of their shiny coats,
While the daisies hum in playful floats.
Together they share secrets galore,
Like whispers of fun in a leafy store.

Earthy echoes—what a grand place,
Every root has its funny face.
Together they toil in joyous glee,
In the big, wild dance of the nursery.

Time's Gentle Hand in the Orchard

Tick tock goes the playful clock,
As time wears its funny frock.
It prances through the rows of fruit,
Wearing shoes that squeak and hoot.

The cherries giggle as they sway,
While whispers of time just drift away.
A lemon shouts, 'I'm sour but sweet!'
Provoking a pear for a colorful feat.

Old man Time shakes his jiggly chin,
As the sunshine breaks through with a grin.
He counts the days like a game of cards,
While the cider barrel rolls with regards.

Five apples later, what a scene!
A barrel of laughs to keep it keen.
In laughter's echo, time takes flight,
Sipping giggles from dawn to night.

Boughs Heavy with Promise

Oh, the boughs are low, not a branch too high,
With fruits so heavy, they ask, 'Why?'
A limb whispers, 'Oh, how I'll creak!'
As the plump pears play hide-and-seek.

A fig looks down, and with a wink,
Says, 'I think I'm more than you think!'
While the grapes insist they're a viney crew,
In this merry dance, there's room for all, too.

With every swing and jolly tune,
The fruits partake in an afternoon.
A joyful dance as shadows play,
Creating giggles in a fruity ballet.

With each promise that drops to the ground,
A burst of joy is what's found.
In this orchard's cheer, we all align,
Among boughs of laughter, sweet and fine.

A Canopy of Unwritten Words

Under trees, secrets flow,
Squirrels chatter, 'Don't you know?'
Branches creak with tales untold,
While apples drop, like jokes of old.

Sunlight dances on the ground,
Where mischief thrives, and laughs abound.
Old roots giggle, fresh leaves cheer,
In this realm, there's nothing to fear.

The breeze whispers playful rhymes,
As shadows leap in funny climes.
Nature's script, on boughs unwinds,
A comedy in every kind.

So gather 'round, let's share a jest,
With all the fruits, you'll be impressed.
In this haven, life's a game,
Where laughter flows like wild champagne.

Threads of Life Amidst the Trees

In the grove, the weavers play,
Spinning stories day by day.
With vines that twist like jokes in air,
And branches waving, free of care.

Fruitful threads in colors bright,
Banana peels slip, causing fright.
A tapestry of laughter's weave,
In every shade, we dare believe.

The owl hoots a punchline bold,
While busy bees buzz tales of gold.
Life's a quilt, a merry sight,
Stitched in joy, woven tight.

With every breeze, a chuckle sways,
As trees join in for silly plays.
Gather the fruits, life's mishaps flow,
Amidst the trees, we steal the show.

Nectar of New Beginnings

When blossoms bloom, the jokes arise,
Honey bees wear funny ties.
Gather 'round for sweet delight,
In this garden, all feels right.

Juicy fruits dangle with glee,
Making smoothies in jubilee.
Lemonade laughter fills the air,
Sipping sunshine, without a care.

Lurking bugs are stand-up stars,
While growing vines tell tales from afar.
The pickled fruit band plays on,
With every note, a new dawn's drawn.

At dusk, the fireflies bring the glow,
A waltz of light, with nature's show.
Raise a glass to quirks and fun,
In this nectar, mischief's begun.

The Language of Fruit and Feather

Birds squawk with witty repartee,
While fruit rolls round, dancing with glee.
Chasing berries like playful sprites,
In this realm, we share delights.

With feathers bright, the crowd takes flight,
As kiwi slices join the night.
A chorus of giggles, the scene unfolds,
Where antics sprout, and laughter molds.

Grapes gossip and cherries tease,
Plums play hide and seek with ease.
In this orchard, humor's the vine,
Where each fruit has its own punchline.

So pluck a pear, and swing with cheer,
With fruit and feather, work the sphere.
In this garden of jests, don't forget,
Life's a joke, and no regrets!

Blossoms of Yearning in Bloom

In the garden, trees wear hats,
With blossoms dressed like smiling cats.
Bees play tag, oh what a scene,
As petals fall like confetti, so keen.

Squirrels dance, with nuts in tow,
Practicing moves, all the world's a show.
They twirl and spin, no care in sight,
While flowers giggle with pure delight.

A breeze whispers secrets, a jest or two,
About the blooms that everyone knew.
They nodded brightly, in colors so bold,
Sharing tales of love, never old.

But watch your step, oh clumsy feet,
For laughter blooms where you dare meet.
A tumble here, a slip right there,
And the flowers chuckle, without a care.

Lanterns of Dawn Among the Twigs

At dawn, the sun spills juice on the ground,
While sleepy branches stretch all around.
The birds awake, with songs so silly,
Each note a giggle; it's quite a frilly.

A chatty crow, in a top hat he came,
Telling jokes that put others to shame.
His feathered friends roll their eyes up high,
For humor is best with a pinch of the sky.

Beneath the twigs, shadows twist and spin,
Where dirt and laughter are twins, akin.
A worm with a mustache, not shy at all,
Rides on a leaf; what a noble call!

So gather round, in this light and cheer,
Where every twig has a tale to share.
In the golden hour, playtime renews,
As laughter blooms in colorful hues.

Roots Entwined in Destiny

In the soil, where secrets entwine,
Roots gossip at night, sipping dew like wine.
They weave a tale of knots and twists,
While chuckling softly, they can't resist.

A grapevine whispers sweet little lies,
Claiming she's the queen, to everyone's surprise.
But underneath all this leafy chatter,
What's really growing? It's just pure matter!

With each tiny sprout that dares to rise,
There's humor in dirt and dazzling skies.
They poke their heads up without a fear,
Hoping to be the bloom of the year.

But watch out! A rabbit hops by,
With a mischievous glint in his eye.
He chews on a root, right in plain sight,
While the others gasp, oh what a fright!

A Dance of Petals and Shadows

Petals sway like hats on heads,
In a dance-off where fun spreads.
Bumblebees bust moves, oh what flair!
While shadows jiggle without a care.

A daisy leads, with a spin and twirl,
Turning frowns to a happy whirl.
And the grass joins in, with a soft green sigh,
As all nature sings, "Oh my, oh my!"

But suddenly a gust, a wild surprise,
Spins the blooms 'til they can't open their eyes.
The wind just chuckles, playing tricks,
While petals whirl like an acrobatic mix.

As twilight falls, the dance slows down,
With giggles shared, not a pout or frown.
Tomorrow's blooms will join the fun,
For every day is a dance begun!

The Promise Held in Every Bud

In spring, the buds all dance and sway,
Beneath the sun, they laugh and play.
With secrets held in every fold,
They whisper tales of fruit untold.

The bees all buzz, a comic show,
They jive around, not moving slow.
The petals giggle, colors bright,
Promising sweets by summer's night.

Awkward squirrels with nutty schemes,
Plotting ways to steal those dreams.
Yet every flower waves hello,
As life returns, and roots will grow.

Through playful winds, the branches sway,
It's all a game, the tree will say.
For laughter's found in every bud,
Life's bloomin' joke, a joyful thud.

The Orchard's Secret Symphony

A rustling leaf, a chirpy tune,
The trees all grin beneath the moon.
With roots that tap along the ground,
The orchard hums, a funny sound.

The fruits all chuckle on their vines,
Spinning jokes like silly lines.
"An apple a day?" one shakes and cries,
"More like a laugh, now that's no lie!"

The rabbits hop with jolly flair,
In a dance-off, no one can compare.
While wormy friends in velvet coats,
Conduct the band from earthy moats.

Under the stars, the branches sway,
As whispers weave in funny play.
Nature's laugh, a sweet delight,
In every note, the world feels right.

Blossoms Under a Beaming Sun

Beneath the sun, the blossoms grin,
With petals soft like cheeky skin.
They reach for rays and stretch so high,
Ensuring all the clouds go by.

The daisies dance, a little choir,
Singing loud to lift desire.
"Pick me, pick me!" each flower shouts,
In this wild game, there's no doubts.

Bumblebees in silly hats,
Swirl about in acrobats.
With every buzz, they spin and poke,
In jest, as nature's laughing joke.

And as the sun begins to fade,
A flower's wink, a gentle tease made.
Life's a hoot in bright colors spun,
Under the joy of a beaming sun.

Threads of Life in Nature's Cradle

In nature's quilt, a patchwork spun,
Each thread a tale, each weave a pun.
Squirrels plotting with nimble paws,
Crafting mischief without a pause.

The flowers giggle, swaying low,
Twirling round in a breezy show.
With nectar jokes and pollen pranks,
Life's colorful canvas fills in the blanks.

Breezes whisper, sharing glee,
As caterpillars munch on leaves carefree.
"Why wait to bloom?" the daisies chime,
"We're here for fun, like all good times!"

In every green, a laugh's embraced,
Nature stitches joy with grace.
In every bud, in every bloom,
Threads of life chase away the gloom.

Echoes of the Ripened Past

Once a fruit flew high in the air,
Claiming it could dance without a care.
A squirrel scoffed, 'You're just a pear!'
And rolled back laughing, unaware.

Old trees whisper secrets they know,
Of apples' pranks and citrus flow.
A cherry once dressed in bright yellow,
Only to find it was just a fellow.

Worn shoes left on the muddy ground,
Claiming they were where happiness found.
'No more shoes!' a peach cheekily crowned,
As worms below chuckled at the sound.

So gather 'round the fruit parade,
Where even radishes join the charade.
In every bite, the laughter laid,
A sweet, juicy joke that won't ever fade.

Branches Cradling Vows

A twig spoke softly to a bold branch,
'Can I get married? I've found my chance!'
The branch just chuckled, 'In a fruit dance!'
While an applekins plotted a peach prance.

Vows exchanged in whimsical flair,
A blueberry slipped and fell from the air.
'Pick me, pick me!' the strawberries stare,
As pears rolled their eyes, not a single care.

Grapes formed a line, hoping to lead,
But a cantaloupe sang, 'Let's all take heed!'
'Best to avoid any fruity greed,'
Said a melon, wrapped up in a seed.

With every union, a laugh would sprout,
Spreading joy without a doubt.
Branches sway, as if to shout,
Here's to love, with no need to pout!

Beneath the Laughter of Leaves

Underneath the laughing leaves,
A grapefruit told tall tales like thieves.
'I was once a star on a TV screen!'
The pomegranate yelled, 'You're just a bean!'

Crisp winds tickled the vines so sly,
A carrot groaned, 'Why must I try?'
'Just throw some puns,' said the spry chive,
And soon enough, they all felt alive.

A walnut rolled to greet the sun,
Saying, 'I'm nutty, but so much fun!'
As leaves chuckled, the seasons spun,
Their laughter echoed, second to none.

In this patch where mirth takes flight,
The produce giggles from morning till night.
So come take a seat, enjoy the sight,
For every whisper is pure delight!

When Blossoms Tell Tales

Blossoms bloom and begin to speak,
Of bees who tangoed at their peak.
'Last night we danced, oh what a week!'
While a rose replied, 'Oh, that was bleak!'

The daisies giggled at the bumblebee,
'Couldn't you see? You hit a tree!'
Laughter spread through the petals three,
As a jasmine whispered, 'Let it be free!'

The violets cheered, 'We're quite the crew,
Making fun of bees, just one or two.
But we'll help out, with morning dew!'
Pledging sweet nectar, what could they do?

With tales of joy, blossoms unite,
Creating a garden bathed in light.
Each whimsy spark fuels endless delight,
As stories blossom, taking flight!

Petals and Promises Entwined

In the garden, a squirrel did spin,
Chasing dreams made of apple skin.
With a leap and a catch, oh what a sight,
Missed the branch, but not the delight!

Bees buzzed loudly, in a mad little dance,
Drenched in pollen, they missed their chance.
One swung by me, oh what a jest,
I told him, 'Stay home, don't be a pest!'

Frogs in the pond, donned tiny top hats,
Ribbiting tunes that rivaled the chats.
They croaked out secrets of daisies in bloom,
While bees swirled around like they owned the room.

At dusk, the jokes turned to simple rhymes,
As fireflies flashed, keeping beat with chimes.
In nature's humor, laughter combined,
In petals and wishes, joy intertwined.

The Orchard's Silent Witness

Old trees leaned in to catch the feast,
Whispering secrets, to say the least.
Lemonade dreams dripped from sweet pears,
While rabbits plotted their epic affairs.

A pickle-nosed dog chased the wind,
Chasing shadows of fun never thinned.
He tripped on a root, tumbled down low,
Got up with a laugh and a triumphant show!

Cherries danced with the autumn's breeze,
Telling tall tales of sneaky little bees.
Every pluck from the branches brought mirth,
As the stars giggled at their shared earth.

Even the moon, with its silver-glow,
Joined in the antics, moving to and fro.
In the orchard's heart, where laughter insists,
The trees stand tall, nature's humorous twist.

Magic of Morning Dewdrops

Morning dew dripped like diamonds bright,
As spiders spun webs in pure delight.
A ladybug stole the day's first sip,
While ants in a line marched, doing a flip.

Sunflowers stretched as the sun gave a grin,
It tickled their petals, beckoning them in.
But one cheeky bloom swayed a bit too wide,
Plopped down on a bee and took him for a ride!

Grass blades giggled, doing their best,
As a bunny hopped through, fluffing its chest.
"Top this, my friends!" he shouted with cheer,
And the whole meadow greeted his leap with a leer!

With laughter and loop-de-loops in the air,
Dewdrops sparkled without a single care.
In the magic of dawn, mischief persisted,
In every pod, a promise existed.

The Embrace of Nature's Bounty

In the patch, a pumpkin blushed deep orange,
Challenging the squash with a wink and a forge.
"Oh please, dear gourd, don't take up so much,"
Said the beans with a laugh, pulling fingers to touch!

Carrots hidden, plotting their rise,
While radishes giggled, disguised as spies.
A tomato tripped, rolled down in a haste,
Yelled, "Ketchup!" and landed with fiery taste!

Cabbage debated the best way to grow,
While basil amused with a wacky flow.
Herbs in a whirlwind, twirled with glee,
Nature's own combos, wild as can be!

When harvest came, baskets overflowed,
With laughter and joy, together they strode.
In each quirky moment, life did celebrate,
As nature's bounty laughed, never late!

Journeying Through the Canopy's Heart

In branches wide, I took a leap,
Outfoxing squirrels, not losing sleep.
With apples grinning, I chase the sun,
Who knew that fun could weigh a ton?

A bird scoffs softly, flies on by,
Thumbs up, I'm ready, oh me, oh my!
Fruits in a race to claim the sky,
Tell me, dear peckers, why even try?

A ladder's my steed, I gallop high,
With laughter echoing, I touch the sky.
Who knew branches could play such tricks?
In this wild world, I gather my picks!

In shadows deep, I find surprise,
With crickets' chatter and firefly eyes.
A jig in the orchard, dance all night,
Till apples roll back, hiding from light!

Threads of Time in Ripened Halos.

Once a seed whispered dreams of gold,
Now it's a party; the stories told.
Around the trunk, we laugh and sway,
In the warmth of sunbeams, we dance and play.

Oh, look at the pears! They're in a jest,
Swinging with wind, they just won a fest.
Singing their tunes, they hold a note,
While I twirl wildly, a goofy boat!

Bananas join in with Capoeira flair,
Threatening to slip—what a fruity scare!
Swing slow, dear pals, it's part of the art,
As laughter repaints every juicy part!

From orchard to kitchen, the voyage is slight,
Messy with pie; what a glorious sight!
Between the laughter and crumbs of delight,
Life's sweeter when shared, oh what a night!

Whispers Among the Blossoms

Petals gossip, flapping wide,
While bees buzz in, trying to hide.
Twirling in breezes, their chatter's a game,
Who's flirting with raccoons? Oh, isn't it tame?

A breeze tickles blooms, just to tease,
While fruits hang silent, oh, what a breeze!
Drop what you're doing, join in the fun,
With peach jokes and giggles, we've only begun!

Each tree's a storyteller, loud and clear,
Tales of mischief that bring hearty cheer.
The apples conspiring, intent to prank,
Just wait till the sun hits their bright, rosy bank!

With whispers and chuckles, dusk starts to fall,
Cackles resounding; we've danced through it all.
Resting in laughter, our secrets abide,
In the hush of the night, with joy our guide!

Secrets of the Gnarled Trees

In twisted arms, a story lies,
Beneath the bark, where laughter flies.
Squirrels plotting, what can they glean?
An acorn ousting a kingly scene!

With roots in whispers, the old trees muse,
Who knew they'd mix comedy with blues?
Unruly branches sway to and fro,
While raccoons play cards in the soft, dim glow!

Nothing like fruit snacks to fuel the night,
Juggling berries, oh, what a sight!
Gnarled trunks giggle, cracking wise,
As shadowy critters behave in disguise.

When twilight paints, we gather in cheer,
Spinning tall tales for the critters near.
In gnarled embrace, we toast with delight,
To the humor of trees that live with their might!

Hope Sang in Dappled Light

Beneath the boughs, the squirrels prance,
They host a dance, a nutty chance.
The sunbeams drop like sticky jam,
While birds debate the best of scams.

A ladybug dons polka-dot flair,
Whispers secrets without a care.
Old gnarly trees share legends bold,
Of acorns lost and stories told.

In the breeze, a rabbit hops,
Claiming victories and veggie crops.
With each frisky leap and bound,
Laughter echoes, joy is found.

So here's to fun in dappled light,
Where giggles bloom, and hearts take flight.
Nature's stage is set so bright,
Let's cherish moments, pure delight.

Kinships of Bark and Blossom

Among the branches, bees conspire,
With blossoms bright, they never tire.
A wise old owl gives cheeky shouts,
While mockingbirds make playful clouts.

The flowers gossip, petals sway,
As butterflies debate the best café.
The sun sets low, the shadows play,
With nature's humor on full display.

A millipede with too many legs,
Trips over roots and then it begs.
Laughter flits from twig to leaf,
The orchard's chat brings joy and grief.

So join the fun in nature's care,
With kinships formed, we're everywhere.
Through bark and blossom, joy we find,
In this wacky world, we're all entwined.

A Mosaic of Life's Flourish

In every branch, a story spins,
Of curious frogs and crafty twins.
With sunlight droplets, laughter flows,
A tapestry where mischief grows.

The grasshoppers throw an outdoor bash,
While chipmunks munch and make a splash.
Frisky critters bid the night,
With silly pranks, they delight.

In this orchard, life's a game,
Where every critter plays the same.
A dance of life where joy is served,
In every twist, nature's curved.

So let's embrace this splendid mess,
With laughter and joy, we'll never stress.
Each moment shared, a vibrant cheer,
In life's grand mosaic, crystal clear.

Enchantment Among the Branches

A raccoon plays the night's best host,
While fireflies dance, a glowing boast.
The breezes whisper silly tales,
Of sneaky cats and flying snails.

With acorn hats, the squirrels meet,
While hedgehogs bandy clever feat.
In shadows deep, the giggles trip,
As every critter takes a sip.

With mischievous eyes, the kittens stare,
At butterflies beyond compare.
As twilight spreads its velvet shawl,
We find enchantment in it all.

So come and laugh with friends anew,
In nature's charm, we're never blue.
Among the branches, life unfolds,
A funny tale that never grows old.

The Language of Silent Fruits

In the orchard, apples giggle,
Peaches whisper secrets, quite the wiggle.
Bananas throw jokes, peels all around,
Cherries burst forth with laughter unbound.

Pears tell tales of sunny delight,
While plums trip over, causing a fright.
Grapes roll around, cracking wise,
In this fruity circus, laughter will rise.

Each fruit's a comedian, taking the stage,
With every punchline, they engage.
The scent of humor hangs in the air,
As vines entwine in a humorous stare.

Echoing Laughter beneath the Limb

Underneath branches, shadows play,
Vegetables crack jokes almost every day.
Tomatoes flaunt their red with pride,
While carrots laugh, they can't hide.

Cucumbers chuckle, crisp and cool,
Dancing with radishes, breaking the rule.
Lettuce joins in with a leafy cheer,
In this garden of giggles, there's nothing to fear.

Fruits and veggies, a stand-up show,
Their humor ripens, ready to grow.
Beneath the limbs, echoes of fun,
A harvest of laughter, everywhere spun.

Dreams Cradled in the Shade

In the shady grove, dreams take flight,
Fruits cozy up, under stars at night.
Strawberries dream of dancing on air,
Kiwi plots schemes without a care.

Plums drape in dreams, soft and sweet,
While oranges plan a fruity retreat.
Watermelons whisper, 'Let's have a ball!'
And nuts crack up, giggling through it all.

Napping under the branches, sweet and bright,
The seeds spread tales of joy and delight.
In the gentle breeze, laughter does reign,
The orchard of dreams, where giggles remain.

Nectar of Memories in Bloom

In the blossoms, memories swirl,
With honey and laughter, they twirl.
Nectar drips with a giggly tease,
As bees buzz by with a cheeky breeze.

Each petal holds a story so bright,
Of fruits that frolic, dancing in light.
Mangoes reminisce on summers past,
While figs tell tales, oh what a blast!

The wind carries laughter on its wing,
As bees gather nectar—sweetness they bring.
Memories bloom like flowers in a race,
In this garden of humor, every face.

A Symphony of Color and Scent

In a garden where giggles bloom,
Flowers wear hats, and bees play the drums,
Petals dance in the light of the moon,
While rabbits tap-dance on the old wooden plums.

Fruit flies chat, gossiping on the vine,
Squirrels in tuxedos host tea parties bright,
Strawberries wink, ripe and so fine,
While cherries climb trees, seeking their height.

The sun is the jester, the clouds, the crowd,
Breezes rustle the leaves, they're laughing so loud,
Nature's a stage, bravo, shout it proud,
Where each little critter plays cheerful and proud.

With a splash of joy, and a twist of fun,
Life's fruity circus has truly begun,
So grab a slice, under rays of the sun,
In this lively plot, we're all number one!

Beneath the Sun

Under the sun, where mischief brews,
Lemons wear sunglasses, sipping their juice,
Tomatoes tease the cucumbers, oh, such ruse,
And strawberries giggle, sharing old news.

The corn stalks play peek-a-boo with the breeze,
While carrots do cartwheels, aiming to please,
Radishes grumble in their prickly tease,
In this jovial patch, worries freeze.

Sunflowers flirt with the buzzing bees,
As daisies gossip about the trees,
The earth's a party, come join if you please,
In fields of laughter, we find our ease.

So dance with the daffodils, sing with the thyme,
Enjoy the wild rhythm, life's simple rhyme,
Beneath sunny skies, we sway in our prime,
Gathering giggles, just passing the time!

Beneath the Stars

Under a quilt of twinkling delight,
Crickets chirp jokes in the cool, quiet night,
Fireflies weave patterns, glowing so bright,
While owls gossip softly, spreading their insight.

Cherries in pajamas have a midnight feast,
Rabbits play poker with snacks as their cheese,
Nocturnal shenanigans never do cease,
With laughter and whispers, their fun's a tease.

Stars are the audience, clapping with glee,
As the moon spins tales of lost bumblebees,
Nature's own theater, wild and carefree,
Bringing giggles and whispers, just like the sea.

So together we chase dreams in the dark,
With a branch as our stage, and fireflies as spark,
Join in the dance, let the laughter embark,
As the moon softly winks—oh, what a lark!

The Allure of Seasonal Whispers

Spring tickles petals, as blooms come alive,
With tulips in tutus, they twirl and they jive,
Buds pop like confetti, in colors that thrive,
While veggies cut up, for a fresh garden drive.

Summer sun giggles, as picnics commence,
Watermelons skate, having fun at their expense,
Berries barter secrets, oh such a tense,
Conversations on ripeness, what a suspense!

Autumn arrives with a playful jest,
Pumpkins wear hats, they're looking their best,
As squirrels do auditions, seeking a nest,
While corn stalks stand tall, feeling quite blessed.

Winter snickers softly, snowflakes make cheer,
Cabbages wear coats, keeping warm, never fear,
Frosted kisses sparkle, spreading good cheer,
In this cycle of laughter, together we steer!

Where Nature's Secrets Are Kept

In a shady nook, where whispers conspire,
Secrets are guarded, beneath roots of fire,
Tomatoes recount tales, growing ever higher,
While lettuce plays poker, a friend to admire.

Mushrooms in huddles share gossip and lore,
While crickets divulge what they've heard before,
Grapes chill with laughter, never a bore,
In the hideout of nature, there's always much more.

Twilight brings mischief, as shadows come dance,
Fireflies unite, sparking up their romance,
Cucumbers giggle, "Let's take a chance!"
Where nature's secrets are shared with a glance.

So gather your courage, join their retort,
In this leafy realm, laughter's the sport,
Where veggies and critters all invite you to court,
In the garden of wit, life's the funniest sort!

www.ingramcontent.com/pod-product-compliance
Lightning Source LLC
Chambersburg PA
CBHW070336120526
44590CB00017B/2913